S0-CJM-377

# Maureen M. Welch

*A biography of a teacher, wife and mother*

by Michael F. Welch

*In memory of Mom.*

*Rich, Mike & Bob*

Library of Congress Number pending.
ISBN Number 0-9705969-0-1

Printed in the U.S.A.

Cover Photo: Maureen M. Welch with her second grade class at Mount Vernon Elementary School, Newark, New Jersey in June 1958.

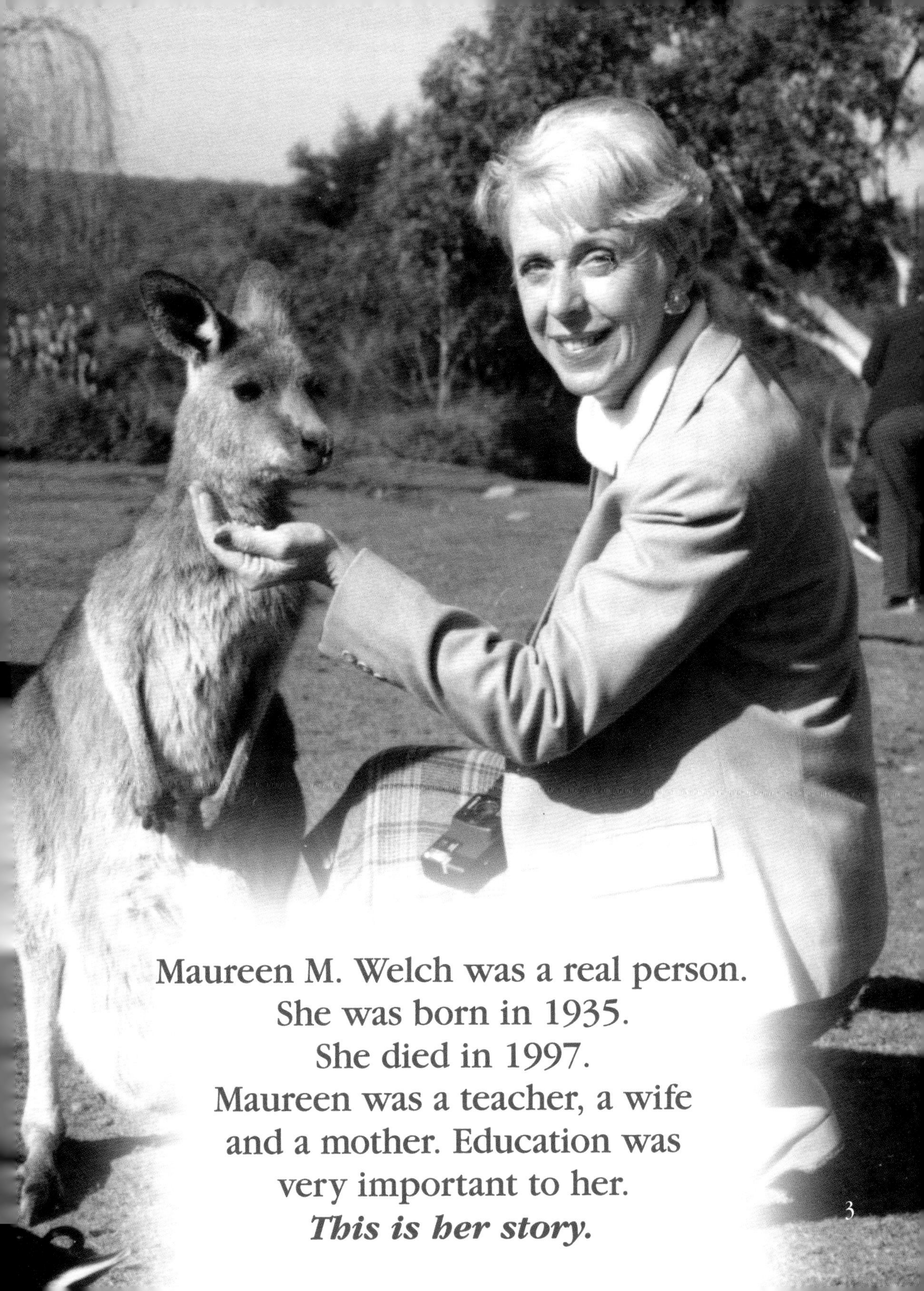

Maureen M. Welch was a real person.
She was born in 1935.
She died in 1997.
Maureen was a teacher, a wife
and a mother. Education was
very important to her.
***This is her story.***

The story begins in South Orange, New Jersey. Maureen grew up in this town and had a happy childhood. She was an only child. Her father was an Italian immigrant named Sebastian Musset. Frances Delaney Musset was her Irish mother.

Her parents were determined to give Maureen a good home and they valued education. But it was not easy for them. Sebastian came to America when he was six years old and he could not speak English. He learned English in elementary school. Frances had eight brothers and sisters. Frances's father died before she was born.

**Childhood pictures of Maureen as a toddler and at age** 4 (above); **Maureen with her parents, Frances and Sebastian** (right); **and the home she grew up in at** 339 **Radel Terrace** (left).

Maureen's parents both went to college, which was uncommon for the 1920s. Her mother was an elementary school teacher and her father was an engineer. They knew that their education had helped them to improve their lives and Maureen's life.

**Maureen in July 1948, age 13, on vacation in San Juan Capistrano, California.**

**Maureen and her mother on the beach at Cape Cod, Massachusetts in September 1946.**

Maureen liked to do things that kids do. She often went to the New Jersey shore with her parents. She started taking piano lessons. And she loved to roller skate. One day she fell while skating and broke her leg!

Maureen learned a lot about America when she drove all the way to California with her aunt and uncle on vacation.

(above)
**Maureen stands on a donkey path leading to the bottom of the Grand Canyon in Arizona, July 1951.**

(right)
**Maureen** (left) **with her cousin, Barbara Mussett and aunt, Estelle Mussett, standing in the Great Salt Lake, Utah.**

**Riding the Snow King Mountain chair lift at Jackson Hole, Wyoming.**

Maureen entered high school determined to do well in her classes. She went to an all-girls school called Marylawn of the Oranges. With a well-rounded education in mind, her parents encouraged her to participate in many activities.

**Hard at work, Maureen** (3rd from left) **discusses yearbook planning with her staff.**

# the authors

MARILYN McTAGUE
*Associate Editor*

MAUREEN MUSSET
*Editor-in-Chief*

ALYCE VILLANI
*Associate Editor*

MARY EDITH VAN RIPER
*Photography Editor*

DAWN LANGAN
*Business Manager*

MAUREEN MANN
*Art Editor*

The yearbook staff at work discussing layouts and planning photography under the guidance of Sister Agnes Virginia, Moderator.

The school yearbook (she was Editor-in-Chief), the drama club and piano study were her favorites.

**Page from the 1952 Marylawn of the Oranges High School yearbook.**

Sodality 1, 2, 3, 4
Class Secretary 1
President 2
*The Marylawn*
Editor-in-Chief
Athletic Association 2, 3, 4
Glee Club 1, 2, 4
Schola 4
Dramatics 2, 3, 4
French Club 4
Latin Club
Vice President 3
Science Club 4
Debating Club 4
Red Cross 4
Seton Debating Club 4
Seton Forum 4
Junior Town Meeting 4

# Maureen Therese Musset

Our hard-working editor . . . always a first honor student . . . sparkling blue eyes and curly lashes . . . ever ready for a good time . . . her congenial nature an asset toward her goal—teaching.

Hard work made Maureen the valedictorian–she had the highest grades in her high school class. She also realized that she wanted to become an elementary school teacher.

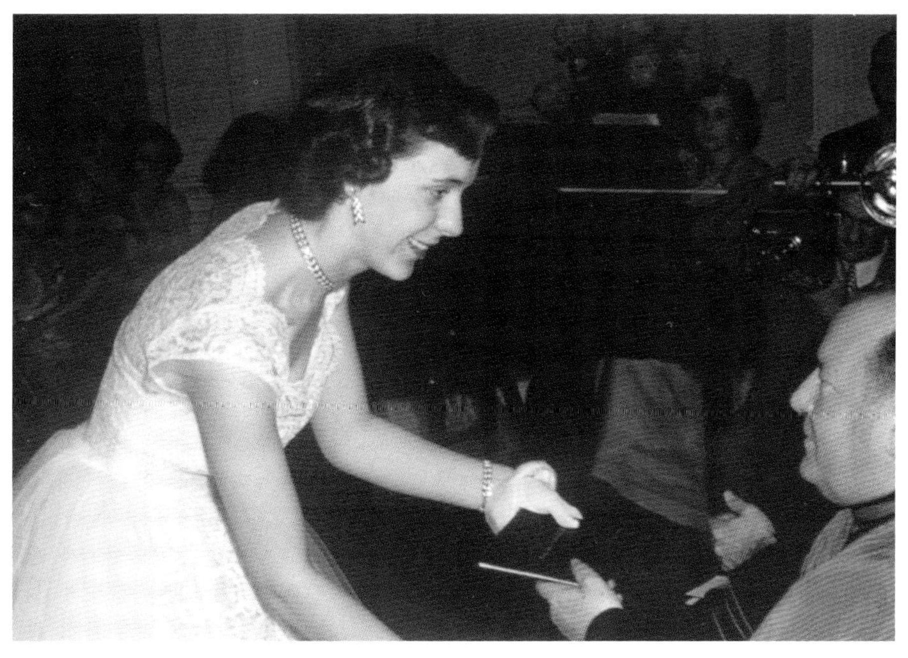

**All of the hard work paid off as Maureen, valedictorian, accepted her high school diploma from the Bishop, in June 1952.**

(left) **Page from the 1952 Marylawn of the Oranges High School yearbook.**

St. Mary's College, an all-girls school in South Bend, Indiana, was her next stop.

Maureen was respected by the other students at St. Mary's and they elected her to be president of the Student Council. She studied for four years to be an elementary school teacher and graduated at the top of her class in 1956.

A gift check of $6,000 was presented to Sister Madeleva, president of the college, by Maureen Musset, president of the Student Council.

## Student Council Presents Money For Frescoes

The Student Council recently climaxed a year of activity by presenting to Sister Madeleva a check for $6,000 as a gift from the student body. The money will be used to pay for the Jean Charlot frescoes in the Fine Arts Building. Through the suggestion of Student Council the money was pledged early in the school year and the goal was attained through class and school projects.

Outstanding achievements and contributions have been made by Student Council during the year. Members returned early in Sep-

tion procedures were worked out and effectively used in the recent class elections. Student Council

**Maureen presents a check to the St. Mary's College President for art-work for a campus building.**

MAUREEN MUSSET
South Orange, New Jersey
Degree: Bachelor of Science
Major: Elementary Education
Minor: Elementary Education

**Excerpt from the 1956 St. Mary's College Yearbook.**

(left) **Maureen en route to St. Mary's College for her sophomore year.**

While attending St. Mary's, Maureen met a young man who was a student at the nearby University of Notre Dame. Soon after their first date, she became engaged to marry Richard Welch. They left South Bend upon receiving their college diplomas, but they could not yet be together. Richard joined the United States Marine Corps and left America to serve at a military base in Okinawa, Japan.

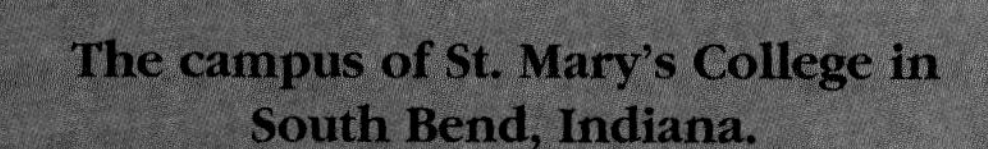

The campus of St. Mary's College in South Bend, Indiana.

Maureen pins Lieutenant bars on her fiancé, Richard Welch, following his June 1956 graduation from the Officer Candidate School at the United States Marine Corps base in Quantico, Virginia.

Maureen addresses the St. Mary's College Student Body in 1956.

While waiting for Richard to return, Maureen started her career as a second grade teacher at the Mount Vernon Elementary School in Newark, New Jersey. She would teach there for three years.

**Miss Musset with her second grade class at Mount Vernon Elementary School, Newark, New Jersey in June 1958.**

**Newspaper clipping announcing the couple's engagement.**

## Miss Musset Future Bride

### *Newark Teacher Fiancee of Lt. R. M. Welch*

Mr. and Mrs. ebastian E. Musset of 339 Radel Ter., South Orange, at a cocktail party today are announcing the engagement of their daughter Maureen to Lt. Richard M. Welch, USMC, son of Francis B. Welch of South Easton, Mass., and the late Mrs. Welch.

Miss Musset is a graduate of Marylawn of the Oranges and St. Mary's College, Notre Dame, Ind., where she was elected to Kappa Gamma Pi. She is a facutly member of Mount Vernon School, Newark. Lt. Welch, an alumnus of Coyle High School, Taunton, Mass., and the University of Notre Dame, is attending the Marine Officers' Supply School at Camp Lejeune, N.C.

They were finally married on October 4, 1958 at Our Lady of Mount Sorrows Church in South Orange.

**Bridal portrait of Maureen T. Musset. She was 23 years old.**

The young couple moved to Churchville, Bucks County, Pennsylvania in 1962. Their family was growing quickly and Maureen decided to leave her teaching career so that she could be home with her young children all of the time.

**Newlyweds Richard and Maureen Welch are all packed and ready to embark on their honeymoon as they begin their life together.**

**The Welch family, Easter Sunday 1963. Richard, Maureen (holding Robert), Michael** (left) **and Richard, Jr.** (right).

**Maureen poses with the boys outside their new fort. September 1964.**

She spent long days at home caring for her three sons–Richard Jr., Michael and Robert. When the youngest was 8, she returned to her career as a second grade teacher at the nearby Churchville Elementary School.

**Maureen with the boys.**

(above) **Maureen with the boys.**

(below) **The Welch family in front of their home at 87 Longview Drive in 1968.**

Maureen loved to teach children to read. She helped kids enjoy reading and she inspired them to be good students. Her job was very important to her. She wanted to do her best, so Maureen studied at Lehigh University in the evenings for several years. She learned how to be a better reading teacher and she received a master's degree for her efforts.

**Maureen Welch received her degree of Master of Education for Graduate Study in Reading from Lehigh University, Bethlehem, Pennsylvania in 1977.**

For fifteen years, she spent her days at Churchville Elementary School, determined to help kids to learn.

Churchville Elementary School

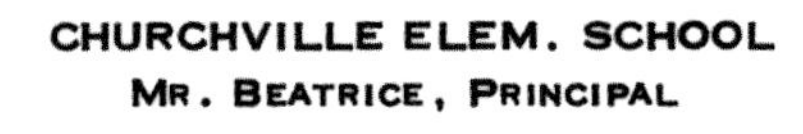

CHURCHVILLE ELEM. SCHOOL

MR. BEATRICE, PRINCIPAL

MRS. WELCH

GRADE 2

1973 1974

Maureen and her husband worked very hard to make sure that their sons would grow up to be good men. They encouraged the boys to play sports. Each son became an Eagle Scout in the Boy Scouts of America.

**Richard frequently helped Maureen during special events at the Churchville Elementary School.**

Most of all, the education of their sons was very important to them. Maureen helped her boys with homework and class projects. She tutored them when they didn't understand a subject. Together with her husband, Richard, she insisted that her sons do well in school and try their very best.

(left) **Maureen's 1975 school photo.**

(below) **The Welch family in 1973 at a meeting of Boy Scout Troop #5, Churchville, Pennsylvania.**

She was proud when her sons later graduated from Council Rock High School in Newtown, Pennsylvania. Maureen encouraged them to continue their education in college. All of her hard work paid off. Richard Jr. graduated from the United States Naval Academy in 1981. Her middle son, Michael, graduated from the University of Notre Dame, just like her husband, in 1983. The youngest son, Robert, went to West Point, New York and graduated from the United States Military Academy in 1984.

**The three sons at Richard Jr.'s 1981 graduation from the United States Naval Academy in Annapolis, Maryland.**

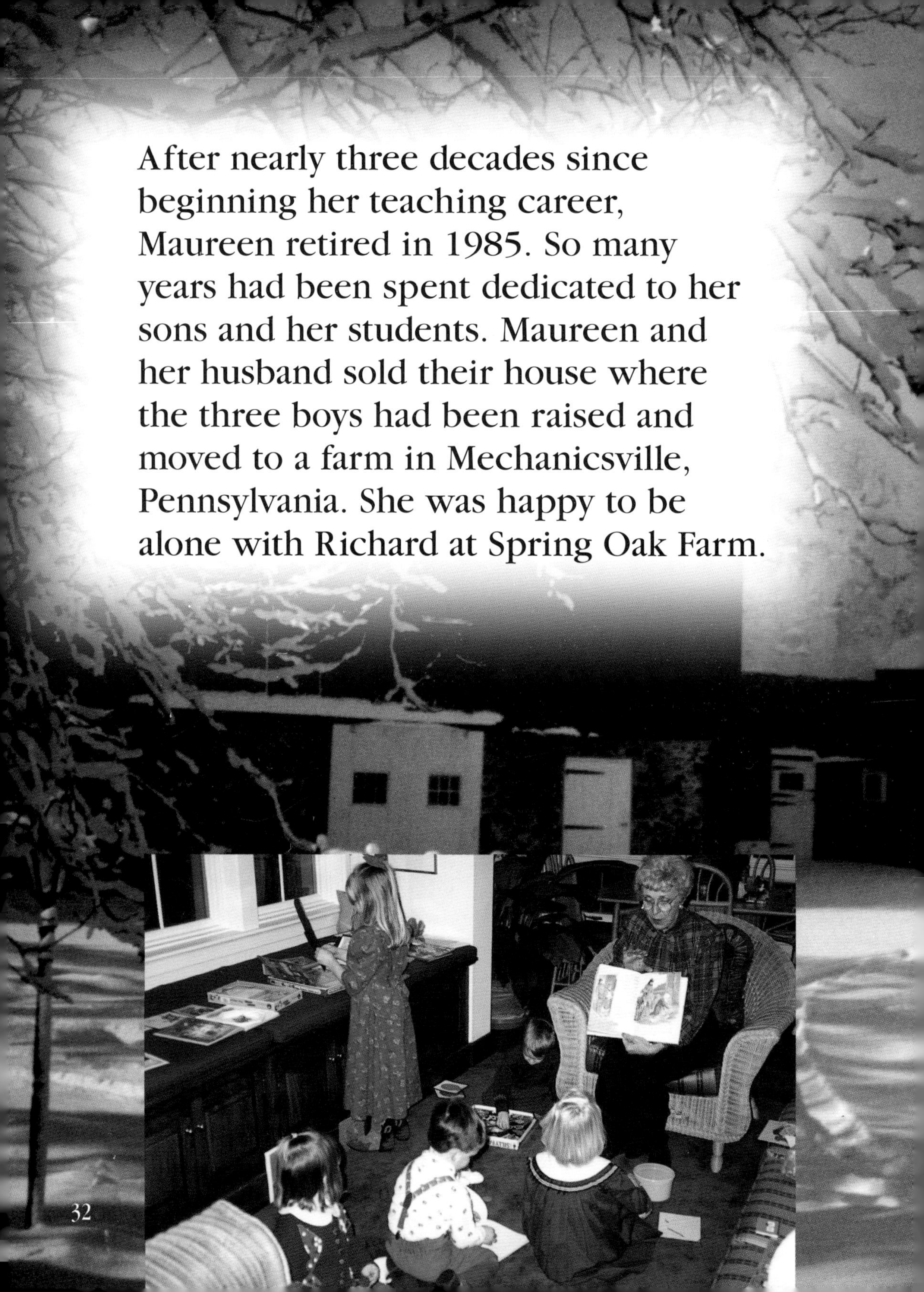

After nearly three decades since beginning her teaching career, Maureen retired in 1985. So many years had been spent dedicated to her sons and her students. Maureen and her husband sold their house where the three boys had been raised and moved to a farm in Mechanicsville, Pennsylvania. She was happy to be alone with Richard at Spring Oak Farm.

Maureen and Richard retired to Spring Oak Farm.

Her retirement allowed her more time to spend with her grandchildren. (left)

It seemed that life became even busier. Her sons had gotten married and she had seven grandchildren. She and her husband traveled to many parts of the world.

(right) **Maureen feeds a kangaroo in Australia while on a family vacation.**
(below) **Maureen and Richard visit Mt. Cook National Park in New Zealand.**

They gave gifts to St. Mary's College and the University of Notre Dame–money that would help other young people to pay to go to these schools. In 1989, she helped her dear cousins, members of a religious community in New York, build a private school for preschool, kindergarten and first grade age children. In 1992, Maureen was awarded the President's Medal by St. Mary's College because of her many years of helping people as a teacher, and as a member of the community.

Dedication of Welch Hall

Thevenet Montessori School
Highland Mills, New York
October 15, 1989

**The Thevenet Montessori School is operated by the Congregation of the Religious of Jesus & Mary. Its young students develop an early appreciation for reading.**

**Maureen with St. Mary's College President William A. Hickey prior to receiving the 1992 President's Medal.**

**Maureen and Richard at the 1992 St. Mary's College Commencement.**

## President's Medal
## Maureen Musset Welch

The President's Medal recognizes outstanding community service and contributions to the life of Saint Mary's College. Since her graduation from Saint Mary's in 1956, this year's recipient, Maureen Musset Welch, has been making such contributions as a teacher, volunteer and loyal alumna.

She has been a leader since her days as a student when she served first as junior class president and then as student body president. Under her administration, the students raised the funds for the Charlot frescoes for O'Laughlin Auditorium and the Moreau Fine Arts Building. She has never stopped being a leader within the Saint Mary's community. Since its inception, she and her husband, Dick, have been active in the College's Madeleva Society, which honors the College's highest level donors. She has served as The Madeleva Society Chair since 1990. She has been a major force in the College's efforts to increase its development efforts.

The Welches have endowed Saint Mary's scholarships in memory of two of Maureen's beloved education professors, Sister M. Agnes Cecile Teders, C.S.C., and Sister Maria Concepta McDermott, C.S.C.

Maureen took the lessons of those respected professors and applied them to her career as a teacher. Since graduating magna cum laude from Saint Mary's, she has taught in elementary public schools in New Jersey and Pennsylvania. She earned her master's degree in education from Lehigh University, and now works with VITA (Volunteers in Teaching Alternatives), an agency which helps clients who request help in reading, English, mathematics or General Equivalency Diploma preparation.

The Welches' generosity has benefited communities in various parts of the country. One special local enterprise funded by the Welches is the Saint Joseph's Chapin Street Clinic in South Bend.

Maureen Welch often gratefully speaks of the time she now has to spend with her three sons and seven grandchildren and with Dick, her husband of 35 years. The stories she tells about her experiences with her grandchildren demonstrate that they, as have hundreds of her students, benefit from their grandmother's love and wisdom.

Saint Mary's has similarly benefited from our association with this intelligent, articulate, gracious and forthright alumna. In turn, as a mother, wife, teacher, volunteer and civic leader, she has always positively reflected and shared the spiritual and intellectual gifts she received while at Saint Mary's.

In recognition of her commitment to education and to this institution, Saint Mary's proudly presents its President's Medal to Maureen Musset Welch.

**Excerpt from the 1992 St. Mary's College Commencement program.**

In 1994, Maureen was told by her doctor that she had cancer. But, she was a strong woman and she helped her family to cope with this sad news. Even later, when there was a big fire at her home, and when her dog, Beau, died, she always smiled and gave encouragement to her family. Her husband, Richard, took care of her while she was sick. Maureen struggled courageously with her illness, but she died in 1997 when she was 62 years old.

**Maureen and Richard with their dachshunds, Beau and Gretchen.**

**Maureen and Richard in June 1993 with** (L to R, middle row) **son Robert and his wife Amy; son Michael and his wife Christine; son Richard, Jr. and his wife Susan; and their grandchildren** (L to R, front row) **Maggie, Robbie, Melissa, Madeline, Kelly, Matthew and Lindsay.**

In September 2000, a new school was opened in Churchville, Pennsylvania. It is the “Maureen M. Welch Elementary School”.

# Sons’ don
# will be na

*Maureen Welch taught second grade in the district for 15 years.*

By Gwen Shrift
*Staff Writer*

COUNCIL ROCK SCHOOLS — A nev elementary school in the Council Roc School District will be named after teacher who lived in Buckingham afte she retired.

The Council Rock School Board vote to name an elementary school under con struction in Northampton Township afte the late Maureen Welch, who taught sec ond grade at Churchville Elementar School from 1970 until she retired in 198 Welch died in 1997 at age 62.

Her sons — Michael, Richard Jr. an Robert — donated $500,000 to the distric on the condition the building be name for her. Richard Welch is a former schoo board president in Council Rock, whic comprises Newtown Borough and Towr

**Newspaper article from *OUR TOWNS* section of *The Intelligencer* on Tuesday, December 28, 1999.**

# on ensures school
# ed after mother

Northampton, Upper Makefield
htstown townships.
d Welch of Upper Makefield and
Welch of Buckingham are the
f Lenape Hall and the Fountain
Doylestown. Michael Welch of
owns the Doylestown Inn.
en Welch and her husband,
Welch Sr., lived in Northampton
for 24 years and moved to
ak Farm in Buckingham in 1986
retired.
roving the school name this
e board debated whether names
buildings would be for sale,
a proposed second high school
to open in 2002.
no one argued that Maureen
asn't a good candidate — she's
emembered as a teacher who
work and whose colleagues and
loved her — at least one board
said he felt many other longtime
should have been considered.
d not look hard enough at people
been in the district," said Chris
He and Warren Hymson
from the vote. Voting in favor
et Smith, Robert Mellon, Bill
Burke, Gail Anolik, Richard Abramson, Cathy Triverio and Jim DiDio.

The recommendation to name the school was endorsed by a committee that included District Justice Donald Nasshorn, Bucks County consumer affairs head Courtney Yelle, Superintendent Tim Kirby and board President DiDio.

Ayoub grilled Nasshorn about how the committee reached its decision, saying he was concerned about "the selling of the name." Nasshorn replied the committee members "weren't looking to cheapen the process."

Nasshorn said the committee felt that naming the school for a former teacher would honor all teachers and that the $500,000 gift would be a good thing for the taxpayers by potentially helping defray the cost of the school.

Richard Welch Jr. said he and his family were thrilled that the new building will bear his mother's name and said she wouldn't have been at all upset by the debate.

"It means a lot to us," he said. "She'd be very pleased with the respectful way the discussion was handled."

Kids go there every day to learn. And there are teachers, like Maureen, trying very hard to help kids find the joy of reading.

Maureen M. Welch Elementary School, Churchville, Pennsylvania.

**Memorial plaque on display in the lobby of**
**Maureen M. Welch Elementary School, Churchville, Pennsylvania.**

## Important Dates

| | |
|---|---|
| 1935 | February 19–Born in Newark, New Jersey to Sebastian E. Musset and Frances Delaney Musset |
| 1952 | Graduated from Marylawn of the Oranges High School, South Orange, New Jersey |
| 1956 | Graduated from St. Mary's College, South Bend, Indiana |
| 1956 | Began teaching career at Mount Vernon Elementary School, Newark, New Jersey |
| 1958 | October 4–Married Richard Matthew Welch at Our Lady of Mount Sorrows Church, South Orange, New Jersey |
| 1959 | Began eleven-year hiatus from teaching to care for her sons |
| 1959 | November 24–Son, Richard, Jr., born |
| 1961 | July 7–Son, Michael, born |
| 1962 | November 4–Son, Robert, born |
| 1970 | Resumed teaching career at Churchville Elementary School, Bucks County, Pennsylvania |
| 1977 | Received degree of Master of Education from Lehigh University, Bethlehem, Pennsylvania |
| 1985 | Retired from teaching |
| 1997 | Died in Philadelphia, Pennsylvania |
| 2000 | Maureen M. Welch Elementary School opened in Churchville, Pennsylvania |

# Index